I0414234

www.providencebooks.net

Publisher Contact

Email:contact@providencebooks.net

Social media: facebook.com/providencebooks

Acknowledgements

The team at Providence Books would like to thank our friends, family, suppliers and customers for making our vision of creating the highest-quality books a reality. Thanks for purchasing and enjoy the quotes!

This page is intentionally left blank

This page is intentionally left blank

'J'eet jet?' is still the standard way for a Pittsburgher to ask if you're ready for a meal, but the meal itself is no longer limited to chipped ham and an Iron City beer.

Bill Dedman

'John Doe' is typically used in a warrant when the accused is known by an alias or by a physical description.

Bill Dedman

A 'Globe' examination found that Boston police officers exercise broad discretion when deciding whether to issue a ticket.

Bill Dedman

A CBS spokesman said the network's policy was tightened in September 2006 to forbid contributions to political campaigns. Previously, there was a bit of wiggle room.

Bill Dedman

A city built on rivers and bituminous coal, Pittsburgh in the '90s has survived the boom and bust years.

Bill Dedman

A foundation representing firefighters who die in the line of duty is calling for Congress to strip the Centers for Disease Control of its role investigating firefighter deaths.

Bill Dedman

ABC forbids political activity by journalists.

Bill Dedman

About 100 firefighters a year die in the line of duty in the U.S. Heart attacks on the job and vehicle accidents on the way to the fires account for about half. The other half are traumatic deaths while fighting fires.

Bill Dedman

After Huguette Clark died in 2011 at age 104, 19 relatives challenged her will, claiming she was mentally ill and had been defrauded by her nurse, attorney and accountant.

Bill Dedman

After a plane or train crash, the National Transportation Safety Board dispatches its experts within two hours. The investigators in their familiar jackets take charge of the scene, secure evidence, follow leads.

Bill Dedman

After every massacre in a school, Americans grasp at quick cures. 'Let's install metal detectors and give guns to teachers' Let's crack down on troublemakers, weeding out kids who fit the profile of a gunman. Let's buy bulletproof whiteboards for the students to scurry behind, or train kids to throw erasers or cans of soup at an attacker.'

Bill Dedman

Although some Clinton biographers have been quick to label Alinsky a communist, he maintained that he never joined the Communist Party.

Bill Dedman

Although the number of manufacturing jobs in the United States has stagnated, dropping 12 percent from a high in the early 1980s, the number of retail jobs has risen 43 percent.

Bill Dedman

America's schools and streets are safer than Americans know.

Bill Dedman

American nuclear reactors are well into middle age. The median age of an operating reactor in the U.S. is 34 years, placing start-up in midst of the Carter administration.

Bill Dedman

An investigation by msnbc.com shows that the CDC routinely takes as long as a month - and sometimes as long as nine months - to visit the scene of firefighter deaths.

Bill Dedman

As more workers lose manufacturing jobs as companies cut back, some are being forced into lower-paying retail jobs. But they still have union cards in their wallets.

Bill Dedman

At one point, Sarah Palin sent her husband instructions to stock up on 'fresh fruit and veggies' for the kids, and 'as little processed foods as possible.'

Bill Dedman

Because appearing to be fair is part of being fair, most mainstream news organizations discourage marching for causes, displaying political bumper stickers or giving cash to candidates.

Bill Dedman

Both CNN and NPR prohibit political activity by all journalists, no matter their assignment.

Bill Dedman

Brand names are well known to business school professors, but only one professor is a brand name herself. Call her Professor Oprah.

Bill Dedman

Cincinnati attracted its first permanent white settlers by flatboat in 1788. It took its name from the Society of Cincinnati, an organization of Revolutionary officers. That name came from Cincinnatus, the Roman farmer and general.

Bill Dedman

Cincinnatians support a symphony, an opera, a ballet, museums, many galleries and theater groups.

Bill Dedman

Cities vary widely in the use of DNA testing.

Bill Dedman

Community groups contend that door-to-door loan sales are often followed by foreclosures.

Bill Dedman

Companies are accustomed to dismissing employees for misuse of computers at work.

Bill Dedman

Disclosure of private e-mails from government officials has been a legal issue in many states.

Bill Dedman

Each year, at the typical nuclear reactor in the U.S., there's a 1 in 74,176 chance of an earthquake strong enough to cause damage to the reactor's core, which could expose the public to radiation. No tsunami required.

Bill Dedman

Even with good maps, there's no guarantee that the public will get the word about landslide hazards, or that state and local governments will take action to discourage or prevent building in dangerous areas.

Bill Dedman

Every scandal has its road kill: the pedestrians who stumble into the headlights of the oncoming 18-wheeler.

Bill Dedman

FEMA says that it does not factor in previous losses into its decisions on applications to redraw the flood zones.

Bill Dedman

Fans love McGwire for his powerful physique, for his on-field hugs of his son, the part-time bat boy. He is Big Mac, or Paul Bunyan in Cardinals red with a white-ash bat instead of an ax.

Bill Dedman

Fans love Sosa for his exuberance, for the kisses he blows to his mother, wife and four children. He is Slammin' Sammy, a fairy-tale figure rising from poverty in the Dominican Republic to the 55th floor above Chicago's Lake Shore Drive.

Bill Dedman

Federal agencies that own bridges have some of the worst records for on-time inspections. Nearly 3,000 bridges owned by U.S. government agencies went more than two years between checkups.

Bill Dedman

Federal regulations forbid delaying inspections for fracture-critical bridges like the fallen Minneapolis bridge - the kind with a lack of redundancy in design, so that a single failure in a load-bearing part can cause the entire bridge to collapse.

Bill Dedman

Firefighters go where they're needed, sometimes ignoring the dangers even when no one is inside a burning building to be saved.

Bill Dedman

For the first six years of his career, Sammy Sosa was one of the least patient players in the game. He could hit the long ball and steal a base, but he was undisciplined.

Bill Dedman

Forty states have sued tobacco companies over the costs of health care for residents on Medicaid and public assistance.

Bill Dedman

Groups that advocate open government have argued that it's vital to know the names of White House visitors, who may have an outsized influence on policy matters.

Bill Dedman

Groups that work in black neighborhoods around the country have contended that much of subprime lending is 'predatory lending.'

Bill Dedman

History is the best guide to the future.

Bill Dedman

Huguette Clark has had her own tax liens - four times, the IRS has filed to collect taxes from her.

Bill Dedman

Huguette Clark was an artist, a painter and doll collector.

Bill Dedman

Humidity notwithstanding, summer seems to bring out the best of Cincinnati.

Bill Dedman

I am not one to seek simple causes.

Bill Dedman

I'm not a person who has people tell me things in parking garages.

Bill Dedman

I'm pretty much a documents reporter. I'm a public records geek.

Bill Dedman

If he is convicted, Dr. Kevorkian says he will die a martyr's death by going on a hunger strike.

Bill Dedman

If police officers routinely issue tickets for the most serious traffic offenses, they'll be treating drivers of all races, sexes, and ages equally.

Bill Dedman

In 1900, the typical American was a boy, not yet a teenager, named John. He lived with his parents and his sisters, Mary and Helen, on a farm in New York or Pennsylvania.

Bill Dedman

In Atlanta, with a large African-American population, Sosa is often considered a black man. In Miami and Los Angeles, with larger Hispanic populations, he is a Latino man, and the black label is rejected as robbing Hispanics of a hero.

Bill Dedman

In Chicago, integrated neighborhoods do not stay integrated for long.

Bill Dedman

In Illinois, where legislators are paid $45,000, plus as much as $10,000 for leadership work, about half are full-time politicians.

Bill Dedman

In Los Angeles, the Police Department buys a 40-foot refrigerated trailer truck every six months just to hold DNA evidence.

Bill Dedman

In Minneapolis, the overhead sky walks protect pedestrians from the winter cold and snow.

Bill Dedman

In Montana, where Sen. William Andrews Clark made his fortune and lost his reputation, people had assumed that all his children were long dead. After all, he was born in 1839 and was of age to serve in the Civil War.

Bill Dedman

In New York, FEMA granted the Mamaroneck Beach & Yacht Club's request to be remapped from the high-risk flood zone in August 2012 - just two months before the club was damaged and its outbuildings destroyed by Hurricane Sandy, which stacked up yachts at its docks like pick-up sticks.

Bill Dedman

In more than 500 instances, from the Gulf of Alaska to Bar Harbor, Maine, FEMA has remapped waterfront properties from the highest-risk flood zone, saving the owners as much as 97 percent on the premiums they pay into the financially strained National Flood Insurance Program.

Bill Dedman

In the Illinois State Capitol, in Springfield, farmer-legislators write the agriculture laws.

Bill Dedman

In the tense days after a powerful earthquake and tsunami crippled the Fukushima Daiichi power plant in Japan on March

11, 2011, staff at the U.S. Nuclear Regulatory Commission made a concerted effort to play down the risk of earthquakes and tsunamis to America's aging nuclear plants, according to thousands of internal emails reviewed by NBC News.

Bill Dedman

In votes cast, Latinos have increased to five million in the 1996 Presidential election, up from two million in the 1976 election. The number of Hispanic elected officials has not risen so fast.

Bill Dedman

It may be no surprise that Pittsburgh has direct flights to London, Paris and Frankfurt, but consider this: many of the tourists here have come from Europe to the capital of culture in the Alleghenies.

Bill Dedman

It's hard to say whether the general incidence of school violence of all types is increasing or not.

Bill Dedman

Jason McDermott can be the most ingratiating young man: a born politician.

Bill Dedman

Jason McDermott's political career, however bogus, appears to have had an early and promising start.

Bill Dedman

John Glenn's father, known as Herschel, was mostly deaf from injuries in World War I. To help out at home, young Glenn sold rhubarb all over town from the family garden.

Bill Dedman

Less than a year after the Sept. 11 attacks, al-Qaida attacks were continuing: the firebombing of a synagogue in Tunisia in April, a bomb outside the U.S. Consulate in Karachi in June.

Bill Dedman

Lie detectors sometimes work because people believe they work, deterring the wrong people from applying for jobs in the first place, or prompting admissions of guilt during interrogations.

Bill Dedman

Like most other states, Illinois has little regulation of the economic interests of legislators and relies on public disclosure to keep the lawmaking honest.

Bill Dedman

MSNBC policy requires journalists to report any potential conflict of interest and to seek approval from the president of NBC News before making any political contribution.

Bill Dedman

Many company policies restrict use of E-mail, limit access to offensive Web sites and prohibit disclosure of confidential information. Few policies, if any, directly address personal Web pages.

Bill Dedman

Many police departments still use DNA evidence the way they have used fingerprints and tire tracks: to determine whether a suspect committed the crime.

Bill Dedman

Many visitors to Chicago know the Loop, the shops on the Magnificent Mile, and the Museum Campus. Meanwhile, much of the bustle is in the developing neighborhoods around the Loop: North, South and West.

Bill Dedman

Mohammed al-Qahtani was not alleged to be a leader of the Sept. 11 plot. He was not trained as a pilot. If he was involved, he was one of the 'muscle' hijackers.

Bill Dedman

More than 30 of America's 100 nuclear power reactors have the same brand of General Electric reactors or containment system used in Fukushima.

Bill Dedman

Msnbc.com identified 143 journalists who made political contributions from 2004 through the start of the 2008 campaign, according to the public records of the Federal Election Commission. Most of the newsroom checkbooks leaned to the left: 125 journalists gave to Democrats and liberal causes. Only 16 gave to Republicans. Two gave to both parties.

Bill Dedman

NBC News found that FEMA has redrawn maps even for properties that have repeatedly filed claims for flood losses from previous storms. At least some of the properties are on the secret 'repetitive loss list' that FEMA sends to communities to alert them to problem properties.

Bill Dedman

New York state ethics rules prohibit lawyers from soliciting gifts from clients 'for the benefit of the lawyer or a person related to the lawyer.'

Bill Dedman

New flood maps in many states have raised the estimation of flood risks along rivers, streams and oceans, adding many properties to flood zones for the first time.

Bill Dedman

Nine of 10 whites in Chicago borrow from top-drawer banks and mortgage companies, which the industry calls prime lenders. They lend to people with A credit ratings, making loans at competitive rates.

Bill Dedman

Nuclear power plants built in the areas usually thought of as earthquake zones, such as the California coastline, have a surprisingly low risk of damage from those earthquakes. Why? They built anticipating a major quake.

Bill Dedman

One-third of all professional baseball players come from Latin America, and Sosa is following role models such as the late Roberto Clemente, a Puerto Rican, from whom he adopted the No. 21. Now he is a model for others.

Bill Dedman

Polygraphs are not allowed as evidence in most U.S. courts, but they're routinely used in police investigations, and the Defense Department relies heavily on them for security screening.

Bill Dedman

Polygraphs have sparked a fierce debate for at least a century.

Bill Dedman

Reggie Campbell and Kathleen Goldsmith are participants in an American success story, the unprecedented boom of home-buying by African-Americans in the 1990s. Only he is black and she is white. When he moved into the neighborhood, she moved out.

Bill Dedman

Relaxing at home in his 55th-floor condominium before a game, Sammy Sosa is the same as at the ball park: focused but funny, exuberant but reserved. He is in a strange country, conversing in two languages, but his every movement displays a combination of confidence and humility.

Bill Dedman

Sammy Sosa grew up without a father in the back of a converted public hospital in San Pedro de Macoris, a dusty seaside town in the Dominican Republic. His father, Juan Montero, died when Sosa was 5.

Bill Dedman

Some employees are protected by union or personal contracts that limit reasons for dismissal.

Bill Dedman

Some parents believe that competition helps prepare children to succeed. Others fear that their children will not be able to handle failure.

Bill Dedman

Spring and summer in Pittsburgh mean outdoor festivals.

Bill Dedman

State and federal laws protect whistle-blowers, those who refuse to do something illegal, and workers who file claims for workers' compensation.

Bill Dedman

State courts usually rule that correspondence between government officials, about government business, are public records, whether they use their government e-mail accounts or private ones.

Bill Dedman

Subprime lending is growing faster in black areas than in white areas.

Bill Dedman

Ted Williams, an extraordinary hitter in his day, has said the swing starts in the hips, and Sosa arrived with one of the strongest lower bodies in the game.

Bill Dedman

The Adversity Index was created by msnbc.com and Moody's Analytics to track the economic fortunes of states and metro areas. Each month, the Adversity Index uses government data on employment, industrial production, housing starts and home prices to label each area as expanding, at risk of recession, in recession or recovering.

Bill Dedman

The Federal Government is achieving its stated goal of helping more minorities go from being renters to being owners.

Bill Dedman

The Federal Highway Administration has allowed states to take advantage of a loophole in federal regulations, delaying bridge inspections to every four years instead of the two years normally required.

Bill Dedman

The Iraq war fueled distrust of the press from both sides.

Bill Dedman

The Manhattan district attorney has closed the well-publicized investigation of the handling of the $300 million fortune of reclusive heiress Huguette Clark - without charging anyone with a crime.

Bill Dedman

The Obama administration is fighting to block access to names of visitors to the White House, taking up the Bush administration argument that a president doesn't have to reveal who comes calling to influence policy decisions.

Bill Dedman

The Secret Service once watched for people who fit the popular profile of dangerousness: the lunatic, the loner, the threatener, the hater.

Bill Dedman

The entire federal budget for landslide research is $3.5 million a year - far less than the property value lost on a single day when 17 mansions slid down a hill in 2005 in Laguna Beach, Calif.

Bill Dedman

The long view of the Census bureau allows some changes that are taken for granted to be studied in more detail. Everyone knows, for example, that people get married later than they used to.

Bill Dedman

The main threads running through the lives of W. A. Clark and his daughter Huguette include the costs of ambition, the burdens of inherited wealth, the fragility of reputation, the folly of judging someone's life from the outside, and the tension between engaging with the world, with all its risks, and keeping a safe distance from danger.

Bill Dedman

The real Representative McDermott said Jason McDermott is no relation. The Congressman does have a son, but his name is James and he does not live in the Midwest.

Bill Dedman

The scientific effort to inform the public about landslide risks often runs head-on into powerful economic interests.

Bill Dedman

The senior thesis of Hillary D. Rodham, Wellesley College class of 1969, has been speculated about, spun, analyzed, debated, criticized and defended. But rarely has it been read, because for the eight years of Bill Clinton's presidency it was locked away.

Bill Dedman

The term 'triage' normally means deciding who gets attention first.

Bill Dedman

There is no accurate or useful 'profile' of students who engage in targeted school violence. Some come from good homes, some from bad. Some have good grades, some bad.

Bill Dedman

There's a longstanding tradition that journalists don't cheer in the press box. They have opinions, like anyone else, but they are expected to keep those opinions out of their work.

Bill Dedman

Though some student activists of the 1960s may have idolized Alinsky, he didn't particularly idolize them.

Bill Dedman

Todd Palin's frequent presence in the governor's office led some in Juneau to call him the 'Shadow Governor.' But it had never been clear, at least to the public, what roles he played.

Bill Dedman

Unlike the United States Congress, which mostly forbids outside employment, state legislatures are generally composed of people with other careers.

Bill Dedman

Wal-Mart has always paid low wages, or, as Sam Walton put it, 'as little as we could get by with at the time.'

Bill Dedman

Wellesley's president, Nannerl Overholser Keohane, approved a broad rule with a specific application: The senior thesis of every Wellesley alumna is available in the college archives for anyone to read - except for those written by either a 'president or first lady of the United States.'

Bill Dedman

What are the odds that a nuclear emergency like the one at Fukushima Dai-ichi could happen in the central or eastern United States? They'd have to be astronomical, right?

Bill Dedman

When Goldberg's 'Liberal Fascism' came out in January 2008, his employer 'National Review Online' announced that Tribune Media Services, which carries Goldberg's opinion columns, had 'nominated' Goldberg for a Pulitzer in commentary.

Bill Dedman

While the House of Blues slogan has been 'In blues we trust,' its stages are usually filled with more reliable moneymakers - Neil Diamond and A Tribe Called Quest among them.

Bill Dedman

William Andrews Clark was caught in a bribery scandal during a campaign for the U.S. Senate - he was said to describe the

Montana legislators this way: 'I never bought a man who wasn't for sale.'

Bill Dedman

With better gear, firefighters no longer surround and drown a fire - they go in.

Bill Dedman

This page is intentionally left blank

This page is intentionally left blank

This page is intentionally left blank

This page is intentionally left blank

This page is intentionally left blank

www.ingramcontent.com/pod-product-compliance
Lightning Source LLC
Chambersburg PA
CBHW061933280526
45787CB00004B/1592